BOY  STUFF

WARNING!
THIS AWESOME BOOK BELONGS TO

_____

Get out of
my locker!

TOP SECRET DESIGNS!

Written by
Sarah Delmege

DO NOT ENTER

First published by Parragon in 2010

Parragon
Queen Street House
4 Queen Street
Bath BA1 1HE, UK

ISBN 978-1-4075-5362-7

Printed in China

DANGER!

BOY STUFF

the most awesome handbook

keep out!

PaRragon
Bath • New York • Singapore • Hong Kong • Cologne • Delhi • Melbourne

Contents

HOW TO BUILD A FORT IN YOUR ROOM!

Forts can be fantastic fun on your own or with your pals!

1. MAKE SPACE!

Move all tables, chairs, and other objects to the sides of the room, leaving a wide-open space in the middle.

2. GRAB STUFF!

Find as many building bits and pieces as you can. Pillows, cushions, and chairs and tables can be used to build.

3. START BUILDING!

Arrange all your building stuff in a large square (or whatever shape you prefer, hey—it's your hideaway!).

4. DOORWAY!

Use a blanket over the opening for a door. (You DID remember to leave an open space to get in and out of the fort, didn't you?!)

5. ROOF!

Use another blanket for the roof.

TA DA!

An amazing fort for you and your friends! Cool!

Here's an awesome picture of MY fort!

Stick a photo or draw a picture here.

I built it on ....

7

Amaze your pals with this crazy mind-blowing trick!

1. Stand next to a wall.

2. Reach your arm all the way out until it's touching the wall.

3. Make your hand into a fist. Make sure your fist is still touching the wall.

4. Hold it there and count SLOWLY to five.

5. Very, very slowly bring your arm back down to your side.

6. Now reach your arm back up to the wall—there should be a space!

Wowza! That's AMAZING!!

The Science Part: This happens because when your arm bends, the muscle in it actually gets smaller, making your arm shrink a little. Nice, huh?

ANIMAL RIDDLES!

LAUGH YOUR SOCKS OFF
AT THIS FEAST OF FUNNIES!

Q. What do you call a three-toed sloth at the North Pole?
A. Lost!

ANIMAL FACT!

Three-toed sloths live in the treetops of South American rain forests!

Q. What kind of jaguar has red spots?
A. A jaguar with chicken pox!

ANIMAL FACT!

Jaguars are tan with dark spots which help them blend into the shadowy forest where they live.

Q. What's black and white and very noisy?
A. A penguin with a drum set.

ANIMAL FACT!

Penguins can't fly, but they can swim four times faster than humans.

Q. Why did the indecisive chicken cross the road?
A. To get to the other side... uh, no, to go shopping... no, not that either ...

ANIMAL FACT!

A chicken can travel up to 9 miles an hour.

Q. Why can't you hear a pterodactyl go to the bathroom?
A. Because it has a silent P.

ANIMAL FACT!

There were lots of different kinds of pterodactyls. Some were small as crows, some were as big as hang gliders!

Q. What would you give a sick ant?
A. Antibiotics!

11

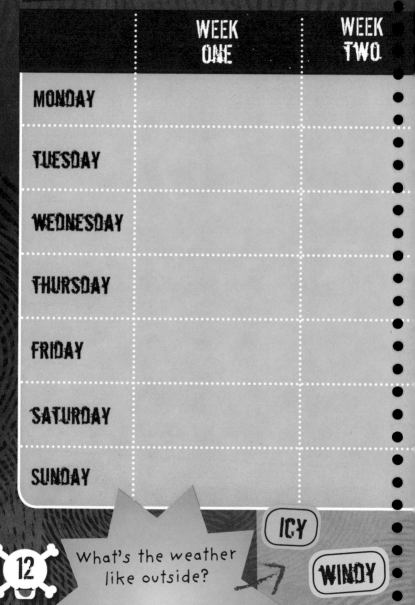

WEATHER TRACKER!

	WEEK ONE	WEEK TWO
MONDAY		
TUESDAY		
WEDNESDAY		
THURSDAY		
FRIDAY		
SATURDAY		
SUNDAY		

ICY

WINDY

What's the weather like outside?

12

Use this handy chart to note the changes in the weather every day!

	WEEK THREE	WEEK FOUR

SNOWY

SUNNY

RAINY

CLOUDY

VANISHING
COIN TRICK!

Borrow a coin from someone in your audience and AMAZE them as it vanishes before their very eyes!

WHAT YOU NEED:

2 coins (make sure they're the same!)

Before you start, secretly hide one of the coins in your shoe.

Now place the other coin in the center of your left hand.

PRETEND to toss the coin into your right hand.

(Really you are keeping the coin in the palm of your left hand)

Close your right hand, PRETENDING to catch the coin.

Open your right hand to show the coin isn't there.

While everyone's looking at your right hand, quickly drop the coin into your pocket.

Now take off your shoe, and there is the coin!

Everyone will think the coin has MAGICALLY traveled into your shoe!

GENIUS!

NAME GAME

See how many words you can make using the letters in your name. You have five minutes!

READY... SET... GO!

Write your full name here:

....

....

How many words can you make

from your name?

17

MY FAMILY TREE

Who's who in your family?

Great-grandmas
....

Great-aunts
....
....

Grandmas
....
....

Aunts
....
....

Mom
....
....

Sisters
....
....

Great-grandpas

....

Grandpas

....

....

Great-uncles

....

....

Dad

....

....

Uncles

....

....

Brothers

....

....

Cousins

....

....

FIT FUN!

Use this handy guide to create a fun fitness routine.

Side Stretch
Stretch to each side, reaching one arm down while raising the other arm up.
Repeat five times.

Sit and Stretch
Sit up tall and spread your legs apart. Lean forward and stretch your arms in front of you.
Repeat five times.

Clap High, Clap Low
Start with feet together. Jump and clap your hands overhead, landing with your legs spread. Then jump back to the first position.
Repeat five times.

Reach for the Stars
Stand tall with your arms at your sides. Raise your arms up above your head and stretch up high.
Repeat five times.

March to the Beat
March in place, making sure to stand up straight. Raise those knees high!
Count to 30.

Tickle Your Toes
With your feet shoulder-width apart, bend at the waist and touch your toes.
Repeat five times.

Jump!
Swing a jump rope over your head. When it meets your feet, jump over it.
Repeat ten times.

OUTER SPACE
MIXED-UP WORDS

Unscramble the letters to match the words that are shown in the box on the next page.

1. ENUTPEN ....

2. ROMEET ....

3. RSAT ....

4. NOITAROLPXE ....

5. URLAN ....

6. RETIPUJ ....

7. ELUHSTT ....

8. SNRUTA ....

9. NSU ....

10. SUNEV ....

11. SUNARU ....

12. STUANORTSA ....

22

13. MASR ....

14. NOOM ....

15. COTEM ....

16. YTIVARG ....

17. ETILLETAS ....

18. TEKCOR ....

MARS   SATURN
    JUPITER   NEPTUNE
URANUS   SUN   MOON
VENUS   COMET   METEOR
    ROCKET   SATELLITE   SHUTTLE
ASTRONAUTS   STAR   EXPLORATION
    GRAVITY   LUNAR

YUCKY AND WACKY FACTS ABOUT YOUR BODY

Gross and awesome facts about what goes on inside you!

The length from your wrist to your elbow is the same as the length of your foot.

You produce more earwax when you're scared.

The average person farts 14 times a day. Phew-ee!

Over your lifetime you'll make enough spit to fill two whole swimming pools!

You're about half an inch taller in the morning than you are in the evening!

It's impossible to sneeze and keep your eyes open at the same time.

You could live for about a month without food, but only a week without water.

Every year, 14 bugs find their way into your mouth while you're sleeping. And yes, you do swallow most of them.

Your heart creates enough pressure to squirt blood a massive 30 feet.

TOP JOKES!

Make your friends laugh their heads off with these great gags!

Q: What colour is a burp?

A: Burple!

HA HA

Q: What kind of dance do you do on a trampoline?

A: Hip-hop!

Q: Where do horses live?

A: In neigh-borhoods!

Q: What's black and white and red all over?

A: A zebra with a rash!

Q: What do ghosts wear in cars?

A: Sheet belts!

Q: Where do horses go
when they're sick?
A: The horse-pital.

Q: How do you get straight A's?
A: By using a ruler!

Q: How do you talk to a fish?
A: Drop it a line!

Q: Why was the broom late for work?
A: Because he over-swept!

Q: Why can't you tell a pig a secret?
A: Because it will squeal on you!

HA HA

27

SEEING STARS

Turn your bedroom ceiling into the night sky with this easy activity.

WHAT YOU NEED:

- Flashlight
- Large empty cereal box
- Tape
- Paper
- Safety scissors

Grab a grown-up to help!

WHAT TO DO:

* Fold the paper.

* Carefully cut small star shapes, diamonds and circles.

* Cut both ends off the cereal box.

* Wrap the star paper around one end and tape it into place.

28

- Pop the flashlight into the open end of the cereal box.

- Close the curtains in your bedroom.

- Turn on the flashlight and shine it toward the ceiling.

- WOO HOO! A ceiling full of stars!

DRAW THE PATTERN HERE

MY STARS
ARE
AWESOME!

ASTOUNDING ANIMAL FACTS

Walk on the wild side
with this pack of facts!

The blue whale can produce the loudest sound of any animal. At 188 decibels, the noise can be detected over 500 miles away.

Horses and cows sleep standing up.

Sharks' skeletons are made from cartilage, not bone.

A locust can jump 2.3 feet. This would be like a human jumping 60 feet!

Insects such as bees, mosquitoes, and cicadas make noise by rapidly moving their wings.

The rhinoceros's horn is made from compacted hair, not bone.

Only the female mosquito bites humans.

Sharks lay the biggest eggs in the world.

Even when a snake has its eyes closed, it can still see through its eyelids.

Despite the white, fluffy appearance of a polar bear's fur, it actually has black skin.

Sheep have four stomachs. Each one helps them digest the food they eat.

The average housefly only lives for 2 or 3 weeks.

Cats use their whiskers to check whether a space is big enough for them to fit through.

INVENT AN ALIEN!

Come up with a new alien and draw it in the space.

Grab a pencil and draw a circle for the head.

Now add a shape for your alien's body.
Connect the head and body with a neck!
Now add legs and large buglike eyes.
Now draw the arms, hands, and feet.
All you have to do now
is color him or her!

GIVE YOUR ALIEN A NAME

Close your eyes and point randomly at the list on the left to choose the first half of your alien name. Then do the same again with the list on the right.

FIRST NAME

Fire
Storm
Terror
Mega
Shadow
Wild
Laser

SECOND NAME

Legs
Jaws
Head
Freak
Slime
Saur
Blast

My alien
is called

....

....

REVERSE WRITING

Use this to write secret messages. Perfect for tricking nosy little sisters!

Can you write backward without looking in the mirror?

Start with your name.

My name is ....

....

My name backward is ....

....

My address is ....

....

My address backward is ....

....

Now write a secret message.

My message is ....

....

Practice your secret writing here

GROWING BEANS!

YOU WILL NEED:

A jar or a tub
4 lima beans
Water
Paper towels

WHAT TO DO:

Put the paper towel around the inside of the jar.

Put the beans between the paper towel and the outside of the jar.

Put a little warm water in the jar so that the paper towel is moist, and leave in a warm, dark place.

Watch over it once a week.

When your beans have sprouted, you can plant them in your garden or in a pot! Make sure they get plenty of water and sunlight!

KING OF KNOTS

Follow these simple instructions to make a bowline knot with string.

- Hold one end of the string in your left hand and one end in your right hand.

- Make a small loop with the end of the string in your left hand.

- Put the end of the string in your right hand through the loop made by your left hand.

- Bring the end around behind the string that's facing up from the loop.

- Put that same string back through the loop. (This time the end is going AWAY from you.)

- Take the top loose string in your left hand and pull the string in opposite directions to tighten the hitch.

- And there you have it. The perfect knot! **WOO-HOO!**

- Stick your knot here.

HOW TO BE A SPY

Try these top spy activities!

SPYING: Find a good hiding place and stay there for half an hour. Watch people and everything going on. Write down everything you see here.

....

....

....

....

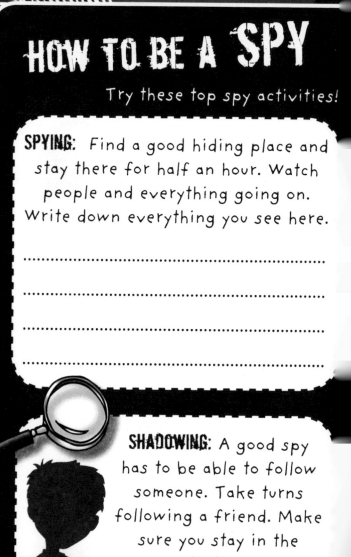

SHADOWING: A good spy has to be able to follow someone. Take turns following a friend. Make sure you stay in the shadows!

DISGUISING: Dress up and pretend to be someone else. Go out and see if anyone recognizes you.

HERE'S A PICTURE OF MY COOL DISGUISE.

39

AWESOME THINGS ABOUT ME

My favorite animal is:

My favorite food is:

My favorite game is:

My favorite thing to do is:

My favorite book is:

My favorite color is:

My favorite movie is:

My awesome friends are:

My favorite teacher is:

My favorite thing in the whole world is:

HOME BOWLING!

Turn your home into your own personal bowling alley.

WHAT YOU NEED:

* Plastic cups * Tape * Tennis ball

WHAT TO DO:

Place one cup on the floor, right side up.

Now put another cup on top, upside down.

Tape the tops of the cups together to make a bowling pin.

You can make as many bowling pins as you like.

Now take turns rolling a tennis ball to knock down the bowling pins.

WRITE THE SCORES HERE.

TORNADO IN A BOWL

YOU WILL NEED:

* 1 plastic bowl
* Water
* A spoon
* Food coloring

WHAT TO DO:

Fill the entire bowl with water.

Stir the water very fast with the spoon.

Drop food coloring in the bowl while the water is spinning.

Now step back and watch. You'll see the shape of a tornado in the bowl!

DRAW YOUR TORNADO HERE.

WOW!

LEARN ALL ABOUT WATER

There wouldn't be any life on Earth if we didn't have water! Read on to find out some AMAZING trivia.

Almost two-thirds of the Earth's surface is covered by water. If the Earth were flat, water would cover everything in a layer two miles deep!

Raindrops aren't really shaped like drops—they are perfectly round!

There are giant waterfalls under the ocean! The largest is between Greenland and Iceland. This submarine waterfall drops 11,500 feet, three times the height of any land waterfall.

Did you know that we are all made up mostly of water? Every cell in our body needs water to live!

Monster waves of over 100 feet tall can suddenly appear at sea when there's no storm to cause them. They are actually accidental meetings of several waves that can combine to form one huge one that could easily sink a freighter.

Water is the only substance on Earth that's lighter as a solid than a liquid.

GO GREEN

Saving water is really important for the environment. Here are some easy ways you can help.

Turn off the faucet while you're brushing your teeth.

Keep a pitcher of water in the fridge instead of running the faucet for a cold drink.

Take a short shower instead of a bath.

TRY IT AND SEE!

BOREDOM BUSTER

Grab some pals and start playing.

YOU WILL NEED:	Some friends An open space

WHAT TO DO:

Get your friends to stand in a circle with one person in the middle.

Have the person in the middle point to someone in the circle and yell, "ELEPHANT," "STATUE," or "AIRPLANE."

He then counts to 10 really FAST.

By the time he has counted to 10, the person who was pointed at must...

...make an elephant trunk and elephant noises (if "elephant" was yelled);

stand really still (if "statue" was yelled);

put his arms out and move around like an airplane (if "airplane" was yelled).

If he doesn't do as he's supposed to, he becomes "it" and goes into the middle.

TOP TIP

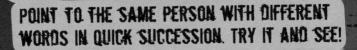

POINT TO THE SAME PERSON WITH DIFFERENT WORDS IN QUICK SUCCESSION. TRY IT AND SEE!

MAKE A RAINBOW

The end of the rainbow is closer than you think!

WHAT YOU NEED:

A glass of water

A sheet of white paper

A sunny day!

WHAT TO DO:

Make sure the glass is filled almost to the top.

Place the glass so that it's half on and half off the edge of a table, and so that the sun shines directly through the water, on to the sheet of white paper on the floor.

Move the paper and the glass until a rainbow shows on the paper.

Q. Jack rode into town on Friday and rode out two days later on Friday. How can that be possible?

A. Friday is his horse's name.

Q. A dad and his son were riding their bikes and crashed. Two ambulances came and took them to different hospitals. When the man's son was taken to the operating room, the doctor said, "I can't operate on you. You're my son." How is that possible?

A. The doctor is his mom!

Q. If I drink I die, but feed me and I'm fine. What am I?

A. A fire.

Q. What starts with the letter T, is filled with T, and ends with T?

A. A teapot.

TRAVEL JOURNAL

Whether it's around the corner or around the world, record your amazing adventure with the help of this handy travel journal.

MY TRIP WAS TO ....

THE DATE OF THE TRIP WAS ....

.... CAME WITH ME.

THE BEST THING ABOUT THE TRIP WAS ....

....

....

DRAW A PICTURE OF SOMEONE YOU'VE MET.

DRAW A PICTURE OF WHAT'S IN YOUR BAG.

DRAW A PICTURE OF HOW YOU TRAVELED.

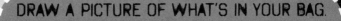

DRAW A PICTURE OF YOURSELF
ON YOUR TRIP.

WACKY RECORDS!

The fastest bird is the peregrine falcon. It can fly at an amazing speed of 168 – 217 miles per hour.

The deadliest disease was the pneumonic form of the Black Death of 1347-1351. It had a death rate of 100%.

The longest bout of hiccups lasted 69 years!

Antarctica is the coldest continent on Earth, where a mind-numbing temperature of 126.9 degrees F below zero was once recorded.

The smallest cat breed is the Singapura, which weighs only about 5 pounds.

Did you know that there's a world record for seeing how many times you can attempt a world record?!

The longest recorded flight of a chicken is 13 seconds.

The smallest dog recorded is a Yorkshire Terrier and was only 4 inches tall.

The longest movie made lasts a whopping 85 hours!

The hottest place on Earth is in Dallol, Ethiopia, which is a sizzling 94 degrees in the shade on a typical day.

PING, PANG, PONG

Try and say it ten times fast...
we dare you!

WHAT TO DO:

Gather your pals
into a circle and
pick someone
to start the game.

He or she must say "PING" while pointing
to someone else in the circle.

The person they point to must say "PANG"
as they point to someone else.

The third person must say "PONG" and in
turn point to someone else.

Keep repeating this until someone
says the wrong word.

The person who says the wrong word
then becomes the judge and is allowed
to try and confuse those still playing.

The last person not to mess up the
word wins!

LETTER PEOPLE

Turn your name into a zoo!

WHAT YOU NEED: * Pencil * Felt tip pen
* Crayons

WHAT TO DO:

With the pencil, write your name on a piece of paper.

Turn the letters into people and animals.

Trace the letters with a felt-tip pen.

Color the figures with the crayons.

Show off your awesome artwork!

55

FABULOUS FIVE

THIS ADDS UP TO A GREAT WAY
TO AMAZE YOUR FRIENDS.

YOU WILL NEED:
Your brain

WHAT TO DO:

Choose a number from 1 to 10 ....

Double the number ....

Add 10 to your new number ....

Now, divide the total by 2 ....

Finally, subtract the
number you
started with ....

Your answer will always be 5!

Try it again here! ....

....

BURPING BOTTLES

This bottle has no manners!

WHAT YOU NEED:

* A quarter * Water * A freezer

* A 1-quart plastic bottle

WHAT TO DO:

Put the empty, uncapped bottle in the freezer for an hour.

Run some tap water over the coin and get it wet.

After an hour, pull the bottle out and immediately put the wet quarter on the mouth of the bottle, covering the whole opening.

Put the bottle on a table and watch!

57

THE VANISHING CUP

Amaze your friends and family with this easy trick.

YOU WILL NEED: A stiff newspaper
A plastic or paper cup

WHAT TO DO:

Tell your audience that you're going to make a cup disappear.

Sit down at a table, facing your audience.

Take out the cup and put it on the table, then place the newspaper over it.

Mutter a few magic words and at the same time draw the paper-covered cup toward you, to the edge of the table, and let the cup silently drop into your lap.

Make sure that the newspaper keeps its "cup" shape.

Now crush the paper, and your audience will think that the cup has magically vanished!

FUNNY FILL-IN

Fill in the blanks, then read the letter on the next page to find out about the CRAZY things going on at your school!

1. Cartoon character ....

2. Toy you'd like to have ....

3. Name of your school ....

4. A holiday ....

5. Friend's name ....

6. Animal ....

7. Something to carry things ....

8. Teacher's name ....

9. Action verb ending in —ing ....

10. Food ....

11. Something you drink ....

12. Your principal's name ....

13. Body part ....

14. Adjective ....

15. Your name ....

Dear No. 1

Please bring me a (an) 2 for my
birthday. You may not think I deserve
it, but what happened at 3's 4
party really wasn't my fault.
You have to agree it was funny when
I put 5's pet 6 in my teacher's 7.
Who could have guessed that the
mere sight of it would have caused
8 to go 9 across the cafeteria into the
refreshment table? The sight of my
teacher covered in 10 and 11 even
put a smile on 12's face—until 8
accidentally fell over and landed on
12's 13. Thanks, and this year don't
bother with any socks or underwear. I
got enough of those last year.

Sincerely yours

15

CREATING FOSSILS

YOU WILL NEED:
Crayons
Leaf

WHAT TO DO:

● Find a leaf on the ground that's recently fallen from a tree.

● Place the leaf on a flat, hard surface (a table will be fine).

● Put a piece of paper on top of the leaf.

● With a crayon, start coloring all over the paper.

● It'll feel a bit bumpy when you color over the leaf.

● Press hard, or your fossil won't show up.

● Once the paper is completely colored, take the leaf out from under it.

● The shape of the leaf will show where it was colored over.

What makes me totally AWESOME!!

I'm awesome because: ....

....

I can do all this stuff really well ....

....

My friends..
think I'm awesome because ....

....

My family thinks I'm awesome because

....

My teacher thinks I'm awesome because

....

Signed..............................

Date...................................

AKA the most awesome boy in the world!

KEEP

ALL YOUR IMPORTANT DATES AND NOTES ON THE FOLLOWING PAGES

JANUARY

1. ....
2. ....
3. ....
4. ....
5. ....
6. ....
7. ....
8. ....
9. ....
10. ....
11. ....
12. ....
13. ....
14. ....

15.

16.

17.

18.

19.

20.

21.

22.

23.

24.

25.

26.

27.

28.

29.

30.

31.

FEBRUARY

1. ....
2. ....
3. ....
4. ....
5. ....
6. ....
7. ....
8. ....
9. ....
10. ....
11. ....
12. ....
13. ....
14. ....

15. ....

16. ....

17. ....

18. ....

19. ....

20. ....

21. ....

22. ....

23. ....

24. ....

25. ....

26. ....

27. ....

28. ....

29. ....

(29 in a leap year)

MARCH

1. ....
2. ....
3. ....
4. ....
5. ....
6. ....
7. ....
8. ....
9. ....
10. ....
11. ....
12. ....
13. ....
14. ....

APRIL

1. ....
2. ....
3. ....
4. ....
5. ....
6. ....
7. ....
8. ....
9. ....
10. ....
11. ....
12. ....
13. ....
14. ....

15. ....
16. ....
17. ....
18. ....
19. ....
20. ....
21. ....
22. ....
23. ....
24. ....
25. ....
26. ....
27. ....
28. ....
29. ....
30. ....

71

MAY

1. ....
2. ....
3. ....
4. ....
5. ....
6. ....
7. ....
8. ....
9. ....
10. ....
11. ....
12. ....
13. ....
14. ....

73

JUNE

1. ....
2. ....
3. ....
4. ....
5. ....
6. ....
7. ....
8 ....
9. ....
10. ....
11. ....
12. ....
13. ....
14. ....

15. ....

16. ....

17. ....

18. ....

19. ....

20. ....

21. ....

22. ....

23. ....

24. ....

25. ....

26. ....

27. ....

28. ....

29. ....

30. ....

75

JULY

1. ....
2. ....
3. ....
4. ....
5. ....
6. ....
7. ....
8. ....
9. ....
10. ....
11. ....
12. ....
13. ....
14. ....

15. ....

16. ....

17. ....

18. ....

19. ....

20. ....

21. ....

22. ....

23. ....

24. ....

25. ....

26. ....

27. ....

28. ....

29. ....

30. ....

31. ....

77

AUGUST

1. ....
2. ....
3. ....
4. ....
5. ....
6. ....
7. ....
8 ....
9. ....
10. ....
11. ....
12. ....
13. ....
14. ....

15. ....

16. ....

17. ....

18. ....

19. ....

20. ....

21. ....

22. ....

23. ....

24. ....

25. ....

26. ....

27. ....

28. ....

29. ....

30. ....

31. ....

SEPTEMBER

1. ....

2. ....

3. ....

4. ....

5. ....

6. ....

7. ....

8. ....

9. ....

10. ....

11. ....

12. ....

13. ....

14. ....

15. ....

16. ....

17. ....

18. ....

19. ....

20. ....

21. ....

22. ....

23. ....

24. ....

25. ....

26. ....

27. ....

28. ....

29. ....

30. ....

OCTOBER

1. ....

2. ....

3. ....

4. ....

5. ....

6. ....

7. ....

8 ....

9. ....

10. ....

11. ....

12. ....

13. ....

14. ....

82

15.

16.

17.

18.

19.

20.

21.

22.

23.

24.

25.

26.

27.

28.

29.

30.

31.

NOVEMBER

1.
2.
3.
4.
5.
6.
7.
8
9.
10.
11.
12.
13.
14.

15.

16.

17.

18.

19.

20.

21.

22.

23.

24.

25.

26.

27.

28.

29.

30.

DECEMBER

1. ....
2. ....
3. ....
4. ....
5. ....
6. ....
7. ....
8. ....
9. ....
10. ....
11. ....
12. ....
13. ....
14. ....

15. ....

16. ....

17. ....

18. ....

19. ....

20. ....

21. ....

22. ....

23. ....

24. ....

25. ....

26. ....

27. ....

28. ....

29. ....

30. ....

31. ....

Addresses

Name ....

Address ....

....

Name ....

Address ....

....

Name ....

Address ....

....

Name ....

Address ....

....

Name ....

Address ....

....

Name ....

Address ....

....

Name ....

Address ....

....

Name ....

Address ....

....

Name ....

Address ....

....

Addresses

Name ....

Address ....

....

Name ....

Address ....

....

Name ....

Address ....

....

Name ....

Address ....

....

90

Name ....

Address ....

....

Name ....

Address ....

....

Name ....

Address ....

....

Name ....

Address ....

....

Name ....

Address ....

....

Notes

Notes

Doodles